Green Apple

Mystery in San Francisco

Gina D. B. Clemen

Editors: Eleanor Donaldson, Victoria Bradshaw
Design and Art Direction: Nadia Maestri
Computer graphics: Sara Blasigh
Illustrations: Laura Scarpa
Picture research: Laura Lagomarsino

First edition: February 2005

Picture credits:
Alamy: p. 31; © Gerard French/CONTRASTO: p. 32;
© Morton Beebe/CONTRASTO: p. 33.

We would be happy to receive your comments and suggestions, and give you any other information concerning our material.
info@blackcat-cideb.com
blackcat-cideb.com

CISQ CISQCERT
TEXTBOOKS AND TEACHING MATERIALS
The quality of the publisher's design, production and sales processes has been certified to the standard of
UNI EN ISO 9001

ISBN 978-88-530-0215-0 Book + CD

Printed in Italy by Italgrafica, Novara

Contents

The text is recorded in full.

These symbols indicate the beginning and end of the extracts linked to the listening activities.

Introduction

The story you are going to read takes place in San Francisco, California. San Francisco is a beautiful city on the Pacific Ocean. It is on a peninsula.

San Francisco is on the St Andreas fault line. [1] This means that sometimes there are earthquakes [2] in San Francisco. A big earthquake in 1906 almost destroyed the city. The last serious earthquake was in 1989.

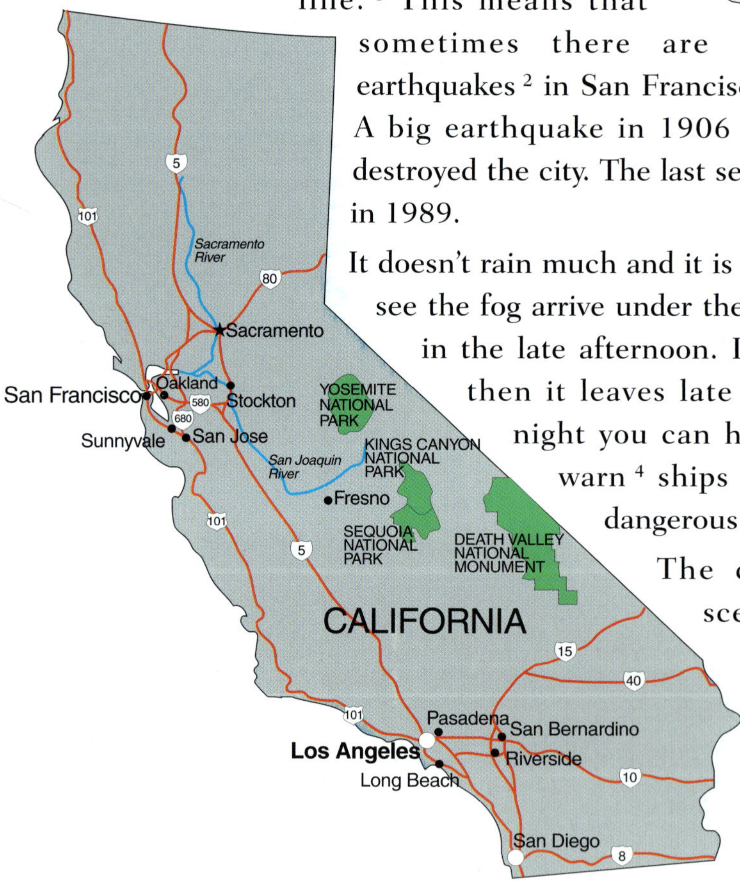

It doesn't rain much and it is often foggy. [3] You can see the fog arrive under the Golden Gate Bridge in the late afternoon. It stays all night and then it leaves late in the morning. At night you can hear fog horns. They warn [4] ships on the ocean about dangerous weather conditions.

The city has beautiful scenery because there are many hills, a lot of vegetation and attractive buildings.

1. **fault line** : a big, long crack in the earth's surface.
2. **earthquakes** : violent movements of the earth. They often damage houses and buildings.
3. **foggy** : when it is foggy it is difficult to see because there are thick low clouds.
4. **warn** : tell someone about something that may be dangerous.

The North Beach neighborhood

North Beach is a traditionally Italian neighborhood [1] with Italian food shops, cafés and restaurants. North Beach was one of the first settlements [2] because it was near the bay. In the 1950s many of the Beat Generation, a group of artists, writers and poets, lived in North Beach. City Lights Bookstore was the center for these writers and poets. Today you can still visit this bookstore. During the Gold Rush, Telegraph Hill was very important because it had a view of the bay. People on Telegraph Hill looked for sailing ships on the bay. When a sailing ship arrived, a messenger from Telegraph Hill went to tell the people. Today there is a big tower on the hill. It is called Coit Tower. A woman called Lillie Hitchcock Coit built it in honor of the fire fighters of San Francisco. Washington Square is a lovely park and meeting place for the people of North Beach. Often there are arts festivals in the square.

1. **neighborhood** : an area in a town where people live.
2. **settlement** : a place where people build houses and start a new community.

1 Are these sentences true (T) or (F)? Tick (✓) the correct box. Correct the false ones.

	T	F
a. San Francisco is on a peninsula on the Atlantic Ocean.	☐	☒
b. It rains a lot in San Francisco but there are no earthquakes.	☐	☒
c. There are fog horns at night to warn ships on the Pacific Ocean of dangerous weather conditions.	☐	☐
d. North Beach is traditionally a Spanish area.	☐	☒
e. The Beat Generation were a pop group.	☐	☒
f. Lillie Hitchcock Coit built Coit Tower to honor the fire fighters of San Francisco.	☒	☐

PROJECT ON THE WEB

LET'S VISIT THE CITY OF SAN FRANCISCO

Your teacher will give you the web-site address. In groups find out information about the following places:

- Golden Gate Bridge
- North Beach
- Alcatraz Island
- Chinatown
- Telegraph Hill

Look at the pictures and read about the place. Then write a few sentences about what you saw and read. Present your report to the class. Who had the most interesting report?

CHAPTER 1

Washington Square

4 Jim Reilly was fourteen years old and he lived in the beautiful city of San Francisco in California. He was short, thin and wore glasses. He had brown hair and blue eyes. His mother died when he was six years old and his father lived in another city. Jim lived with his grandfather. This was his first year in high school and he liked it a lot. His favorite subject was science. On weekends he had a part-time job at a supermarket to make extra pocket money.[1]

Jim's home was on Telegraph Hill near San Francisco Bay. From his living room he could see the Golden Gate Bridge and the bay. Every morning he walked down Telegraph Hill. He met his friends at the bus stop at Washington Square. They went to high school together.

Washington Square was a historical landmark and the people of San Francisco loved to go there. It was a lovely park for children

1. **pocket money** : a small amount of money to buy personal things.

and adults. There was a small playground for children. It was also a place for the people of the North Beach neighborhood to meet. There were restaurants, cafés and nice shops around Washington Square. Often there were music and arts festivals.

Normally, Washington Square had green grass and beautiful flowers. But there was no rain for a long time, and the grass was dry and yellow and the flowers were dead.

"Hi, Jim," said Brian. Brian Wilson was Jim's best friend. He was fourteen too. He was a tall boy, with blond, curly hair and green eyes. He played basketball on the high school team. His parents had a grocery store [1] and he helped them on weekends.

"Hi, Brian. Did you finish your English homework?" said Jim.

"Yes, I did, but Shakespeare wasn't easy. Look, there's Susan," said Brian.

"Hi, guys," said Susan. Susan Hardy was a pretty African-American girl. She was a good friend of both boys. She was also a very good student. She had a part-time job as a babysitter for the children of her neighbors, the Moreno family. Her brother Tom was twenty years old. He was a biology student at San Francisco University and played on the university football team.

"Are you ready for the math test?" asked Susan.

"I studied all afternoon yesterday, but I'm not ready," said Brian.

"I'm not either. I didn't look at my notes," said Jim.

The bus came and they got on. They saw their school friends and started talking. The bus was always crowded, [2] but the bus ride was fun. When they got near Galileo High School they could smell

1. **grocery store** : a place to buy food and drinks.
2. **crowded** : full of people.

the chocolate from the chocolate factory [1] nearby. They loved the smell of the chocolate. It made them hungry.

The math test was difficult. The students were happy when it was finally lunchtime. They all went to the big school cafeteria.

"Why is math so difficult?" said Jim. "I think Mrs Miller makes the test difficult."

"Don't worry about the test and eat your lunch," said Brian.

In the afternoon they had a long science lesson. It was very interesting. They studied chemistry in the school laboratory. They often did experiments with their chemistry teacher, Mr Woods. They liked Mr Woods.

At a quarter past three the school bell rang. It was time to go home and it was Friday.

"What are you doing this weekend?" asked Brian.

"I'm working at the supermarket tomorrow," said Jim. "But on Sunday I'm coming to see your basketball game."

"I hope we win," said Brian. "I'm working tomorrow as well, at my parents' grocery store. It's always a busy day. But I'm free tomorrow night."

"Well, I'm babysitting for the Moreno children all weekend," said Susan.

"Do you want to go to the movies tomorrow night, Jim?" asked Brian.

"Yes, that's a great idea," said Jim. "I'll phone you."

1. **factory** : building where things are made, usually in big quantities.

13

UNDERSTANDING THE TEXT

KET

1 **Are these sentences "Right" (A) or "Wrong" (B)? If there is not enough information to answer "Right" or "Wrong", choose "Doesn't say" (C). There is an example at the beginning (0).**

0 Jim Reilly lives in San Francisco with his grandmother.
A Right　　B Wrong　　C Doesn't say

1 He works in a supermarket on weekends.
A Right　　B Wrong　　C Doesn't say

2 Washington Square is very big.
A Right　　B Wrong　　C Doesn't say

3 Washington Square is always very busy in the evenings.
A Right　　B Wrong　　C Doesn't say

4 Brian plays football on the high school team.
A Right　　B Wrong　　C Doesn't say

5 Susan Hardy is one of Jim and Brian's friends.
A Right　　B Wrong　　C Doesn't say

6 Mr Woods always gives the students a lot of homework.
A Right　　B Wrong　　C Doesn't say

7 Brian's parents have a supermarket.
A Right　　B Wrong　　C Doesn't say

2 **SCHOOL SUBJECTS**

Complete the sentences with the correct school subject from the box.

math	geography	history	science	English

a. In geography you study where places are.
b. In English you study language and literature.
c. In science you study the natural things around us.
d. In history you study what happened in the past.
e. In math you study numbers and shapes.

What subjects do you study at school? Make a list and write definitions for each one.

3 CHARACTERS

Look at the picture of Susan, Jim and Brian. Can you describe them? Use the words in the box below to write some sentences about each person.

African-American	blond, curly hair	blue eyes	brown hair	
glasses	green eyes	pretty	short	tall, thin, brown eyes

a. Susan: She is a African - American Girl, she has brown eyes and a pretty face

b. Jim: ....

c. Brian: ....

Now describe someone you know.

T: GRADE 3

4 SPEAKING

Topic – Jobs

Jim has a part-time job at a supermarket. Susan sometimes works as a babysitter. Brian works in his parents' grocery store. Bring in a picture of a job that interests you. Tell your class about the job. Use these questions to help you.

a. What kind of job do you want to do?
b. What do you like about this job?
c. What subjects do you need to study to do this job?
d. At what age can you start to work in your country?

BEFORE YOU READ

1 **Match the words to what you can see in the picture.**

1. ☐ mansion
2. ☐ fence
3. ☐ gate
4. ☐ ghost
5. ☐ garden
6. ☐ bat
7. ☐ pond
8. ☐ duck

CHAPTER 2

The Face at the Window

5 Jim walked slowly up Telegraph Hill. It was a foggy afternoon in February. Every day Jim walked in front of an old mansion. It was a mysterious wooden building with a big garden and a fence around it.

Jim often looked at it and thought, "What's inside? Why doesn't anyone live here?" That afternoon he stopped in front of the gate. He looked at the garden and the trees. What a strange place. No one took care of it. Then he looked up at the old mansion. He looked at the window on the second floor. There was a face behind it. He felt cold. It was the face of a little girl with long, dark hair. But no one lived in that mansion. Who was it? A ghost?

Jim didn't believe in ghosts, but *who* was the girl at the window? She looked down at him. He continued looking at the window. Suddenly the face of the girl disappeared.

Jim could not see well because it was very foggy. He decided to go home quickly.

He walked in the door and into the living room. He saw his grandfather in the corner of the room.

"Grandpa!" he cried "I saw a ghost!"

"*What* did you say?" asked his grandfather with a smile.

"I saw the face of a little girl at the window of the old mansion. No one lives there, but I saw a girl. She looked at me!"

"Are you sure, Jim? It's a very foggy afternoon. Did you see her clearly? No one lives in the old Stewart mansion. It's about one hundred years old. There's a strange story about it, but I don't think there are any ghosts."

"What story? Please tell me!" said Jim.

"Well, Mr Stewart was a very rich, but very strange man. He was very interested in science and experiments. He had a lot of enemies.[1] People thought his experiments were mysterious and sinister.[2] His wife and daughter died in a mysterious accident. It was terrible. He left San Francisco and returned to New York."

"I saw a face, grandpa – I did!" said Jim.

"But, Jim, you don't believe in ghosts," said his grandfather.

"You're right – but I saw that girl's face," said Jim.

"Maybe it was your imagination," said his grandfather kindly.

Jim went to his room and turned on the radio. He listened to some songs and then started doing his homework.

The next day Jim went to work at the supermarket. It was a busy day. A strange man with long hair and a silver earring[3] came in. His clothes were old. Customers were usually friendly but this man was

1. **enemies** : the opposite of friends.
2. **sinister** : bad.
3. **silver earring** : 

not. He had an angry expression, paid quickly and left. There was something strange about him.

When Jim went home that evening he phoned Brian.

"Hi. How was your day?"

"Very busy," said Brian.

"Yes, mine too. Do you want to see that new science fiction movie on at The Big Screen movie theater? We can meet at 7 p.m. in front of the park," said Jim.

"OK. I'll see you then," said Brian, "at Washington Square."

"Don't be late."

Jim left the house and started walking to the park. He stopped in front of the gate of the old Stewart mansion again. There was no one at the window. He stayed there a few minutes. It was windy and the big trees in the garden made strange noises. [1] He looked at his watch. It was nearly seven o'clock. He was late to meet Brian.

1. **noises** : sounds.

UNDERSTANDING THE TEXT

1 Choose the correct answer A, B or C.

1. The Stewart mansion was
   A about 100 years old.
   B very modern.
   C in Washington Square.
2. Jim saw the face of
   A a teenage girl.
   B a young girl.
   C old Mr Stewart.
3. Mr Stewart was a
   A poor scientist.
   B rich, kind man.
   C rich, but strange man.
4. Brian and Jim wanted to see
   A a science fiction movie.
   B a thriller.
   C a romantic movie.
5. They decided to meet
   A near Brian's house.
   B in front of the high school.
   C in Washington Square.
6. Jim was
   A early to meet Brian.
   B late to meet Brian.
   C on time to meet Brian.

2 TELLING THE TIME

Write the times in numbers and words.

a. ...half past nine......

...9.30....

b. ....

....

c. ....

....

d. ....

....

e. ....

....

f. ....

....

3 Now listen to five short conversations. What times do you hear? Choose from the clocks (a-f).

1. ☐ 2. ☐ 3. ☐ 4. ☐ 5. ☐

4

SPEAKING

What do you do everyday? Think of ten things you do everyday? Talk with a partner and tell him or her what you do and what time you do it. You can use some of the events in the box to help you.

wake up | get up | have breakfast | brush teeth
have a shower or bath | get dressed | go to school or work
catch a bus/train | have lunch | go home
play football/tennis/basketball | go swimming/jogging
play a musical instrument | do homework | have dinner
wash the dishes | turn on the television | go to bed

5

OPPOSITES

Match the words on the left with their opposites on the right.

1. ☐ rich
2. ☐ enemies
3. ☐ late
4. ☐ old
5. ☐ quick
6. ☐ cold
7. ☐ big
8. ☐ long

a. small
b. new
c. slow
d. hot
e. friends
f. early
g. poor
h. short

Write four sentences using one of the words from the list for each sentence.

Example: Mr Stewart was a rich man.

1. ....
2. ....
3. ....
4. ....

CHAPTER 3

The Stewart Mansion

After the movies the two boys went to eat an ice-cream at Pier 39. It was a beautiful night. They stopped and looked at Alcatraz Island in the middle of San Francisco Bay.

Jim told Brian about the face at the window.

"What?" said Brian. "I don't believe it. I want to come with you next week. I want to see her too."

"Really? That's great," said Jim. "It's a strange place. I'm always a little afraid when I go alone. Let's go together soon."

On Monday after school the two friends met Susan at the bus stop. They got on the bus.

"Where are you going?" Susan asked.

"Can you keep a secret?" asked Jim.

"Why? Do you have a secret?" asked Susan.

"Yes, I do," said Jim.

"Is it about Jenny Lee's new boyfriend?" asked Susan. Jenny was a

PIER 39

very popular girl in their class. Susan hoped Jenny Lee's new boyfriend wasn't Jim.

He told her about the Stewart mansion and about the face at the window. Then he told his friends his grandfather's story about the mansion, the scientist and the mysterious accident.

"Scary!" said Susan. "Old mansions always have ghosts. Can I come with you?"

Jim smiled at her and said, "Of course, but promise not to tell anyone." Jim was happy that Susan wanted to come. Susan was pretty.

"Hey, come on, it's our stop," said Brian. "Let's get off."

It was 4.30 p.m. and it was a cold, sunny afternoon. The three friends walked up Telegraph Hill. When they arrived at the Stewart mansion they stopped in front of the old gate.

"What a strange place," said Susan.

"It's cool!" [1] said Brian.

They looked at the window on the second floor but they saw nothing.

They started talking and looking around.

"Hey, do you smell anything strange?" said Susan.

They stopped and smelled the air. There was a very bad smell in the air.

"What is that smell?" asked Brian.

"I don't know. It smells like rotten eggs!" [2] said Jim.

"Yes, that's true. But where is it coming from?" asked Brian.

Susan and Brian looked at Jim. Then they looked at the window on the second floor again.

1. **It's cool** : (here) I like it.
2. **rotten eggs** : eggs that are bad.

The Stewart Mansion

"Are you sure you saw a face, Jim?" asked Susan.

Jim didn't know what to say. There was no one at the window now.

"This is a scary place but I don't see any ghosts," said Brian.

"This smell is terrible," said Susan. "Let's go home and forget about the ghost. It was probably your imagination, Jim."

"Look!" cried Jim. "There's yellow smoke over there." Near the bottom window of the mansion they saw strange yellow smoke in the air.

"Wow! You're right," said Susan.

"What's happening here?" said Brian.

"It smells like a dead body. Maybe there's a dead body in the mansion! Maybe this is a secret cemetery," said Jim.

Brian's face became white. The three friends looked at each other.

"A secret cemetery?"[1] they said softly.

They were curious but terrified at the same time. No one knew what to say.

"Oh, please let's go home. This place frightens me," said Susan.

"There's something strange happening here," said Brian.

They agreed to leave, and went to Jim's house to listen to his new CDs. They sat in Jim's room and talked about the mansion.

Then Susan suddenly said, "Hey, there's the big Chinese New Year parade this Saturday night. I'm taking the Moreno children."

"It's always lots of fun," said Jim. "I'm going to go."

"Me too," said Brian.

1. **cemetery** : 

UNDERSTANDING THE TEXT

1 **Complete the following sentences. Choose from the endings (a-f).**

1. ☐ Jim and Brian went to eat an ice-cream
2. ☐ Jenny Lee was
3. ☐ They looked at the window on the second floor
4. ☐ There was yellow smoke
5. ☐ Susan wanted to go home
6. ☐ The Chinese New Year parade was

a. but they saw nothing.
b. near the bottom window of the mansion.
c. because she was frightened.
d. after the movie.
e. on Saturday night.
f. very popular.

2 **SUMMARY**

Use the verbs in the box to complete this summary of Chapter Three. You will need to put some of the verbs in the Past Simple form. Be careful, some of the verbs have irregular Past Simple forms.

be (x 2)	decide	go	look	see (x 2)	smell
stop	~~tell~~	understand			

Jim 0....told........ Brian about the face at the window. When they 1................. Susan, they 2................. to tell her too. So, on Monday after school they all decided to 3................. and see the mansion. When they arrived at the Stewart mansion they 4................. in front of the old gate. They 5................. at the window on the second floor, but the little girl 6................. not there. There was a horrible smell in the air. It 7................. like rotten eggs. Then they 8................. some yellow smoke coming from one of the windows of the mansion.
Jim, Brian and Susan didn't 9................. . They were very curious, but they 10................. also afraid.

KET

3 **Complete the conversation. What does Susan say to Brian? Write the correct letter next to the number.**

Brian: Do you want to go to the Chinese New Year parade?
Susan: 0 ....E............
Brian: What time do you want to go?
Susan: 1 ....
Brian: Jim is coming too.
Susan: 2 ....
Brian: Do you want to take the cable car to Chinatown?
Susan: 3 ....
Brian: OK. Is your brother coming with us?
Susan: 4 ....
Brian: Where is he going?
Susan: 5 ....

A At about half past eight.
B No, let's walk.
C No, he doesn't.
D He's going to a football game.
E Yes, let's go.
F Yes, I am.
G No, he can't come.
H Great!

T: GRADE 3

4 **SPEAKING**

Topic – Free time

In their free time Jim, Brian and Susan like listening to CDs, going to the movies, eating ice-cream on Pier 39 and sometimes they like going to the Stewart Mansion.

What do you like doing in your free time? Think of three things you like doing and talk about them to the class. Use these questions to help you.

a. What three things are you going to talk about?
b. When do you do these things?
c. Why do you like them?
d. Are they easy or difficult to do?

A Guide to San Francisco

8 San Francisco is an international center for business, education, science and the arts. Thousands of tourists visit the city every year because there are many interesting places to see.

San Francisco is a very cosmopolitan city; people from all over the world live there. There are a lot of multicultural neighborhoods.

Chinatown is a very big, colorful Chinese neighborhood on Grant Avenue. The streets here are narrow. There are Chinese food shops, souvenir shops and restaurants. There are also Chinese libraries and Chinese schools. Many children from Chinese families go to Chinese school after regular school. They want to learn to speak, read and write their parents' language. The street signs and shop signs in Chinatown are in Chinese too.

The entrance into Chinatown.

A view of Alcatraz Island from above.

Alcatraz Island is a small island in San Francisco bay. It is a big tourist attraction because it was a famous prison for many years. There was one guard for every three to five prisoners. Some prisoners tired to escape but they failed. [1] It was impossible to escape from Alcatraz by swimming across to San Francisco because of the cold water. Alcatraz was home to many dangerous criminals like the gangster [2] Al Capone.

The prison was closed in 1963 because the conditions were very bad. Now it is a museum. You can see photographs of some of the prisoners there and read about them. There are many exciting movies about Alcatraz Island and its prisoners.

Pier 39 is another famous attraction on the bay. There are many different shops, games galleries, ice-cream stands and entertainments on the pier. Many of the shops sell funny T-shirts.

1. **failed** : could not do it.
2. **gangster** : member of a violent group of criminals.

Fisherman's Wharf is on the bay, too. There are hundreds of fishing boats and outdoor food stands with good seafood. There are also many street artists and souvenir shops. At Fisherman's Wharf you can take an exciting boat ride on the bay. Remember to wear warm clothes because it's sometimes very windy on the bay.

The cable car is a common form of transportation in San Francisco. It climbs up and down the city's hills. It is great fun to ride the cable car.

Golden Gate Park is a big park in the middle of the city. There are many excellent museums, a famous aquarium and a flower conservatory.[1] You

1. **conservatory** : (here) building you can visit to see lots of flowers.

Cable cars traveling up and down the hills.

can also ride your bike or go jogging in this beautiful park. A great symbol of San Francisco is the Golden Gate Bridge. It is a spectacular bridge with its red-orange color. It was very difficult to build it in 1937, because of the strong winds and rough [1] sea. It connects San Francisco to northern California. Another bridge connects the city to eastern California. This is called the Bay Bridge.

Union Square is in the city center. It is an international shopping area with many famous designer shops and big department stores.

There are many tall buildings in the center of San Francisco. They are called skyscrapers. One skyscraper looks like a giant triangle.

The weather in San Francisco is often foggy and windy, it doesn't rain a lot. A lot of people go to live in San Francisco because it has so many attractions. The people of San Francisco are very popular in America because they are usually very friendly and outgoing. [2]

A view of the San Francisco skyline.

1. **rough** : (here) violent, dangerous.
2. **outgoing** : sociable. Enjoy being with other people.

1 **Complete the notes about each of the places below.**

Chinatown

a. The main area is on ....

b. There are many Chinese ...., ... and .... in the area.

Alcatraz

c. It is a tourist attraction because there was .... on the island.

d. Impossible to escape because of ....

e. .... was one of the prisoners on the island.

f. It closed in ....

Fisherman's Wharf

g. You can find a lot of .... here.

h. An exciting .... around the bay leaves from here.

Golden Gate Bridge

i. The bridge is a .... color.

j. When the people built it in ...., they had many problems because of the .... and ....

BEFORE YOU READ

1 **Listen to the first part of Chapter Four. Are the following sentences true (T) or false (F)?**

9

		T	F
1.	Many people go to see the Chinese New Year parade.	☐	☐
2.	Jim and Brian took the bus to Grant Avenue.	☐	☐
3.	Jenny Lee's boyfriend was the captain of the football team.	☐	☐
4.	Susan was at the parade.	☐	☐
5.	The little girl played with the big paper dragon.	☐	☐
6.	Jim and Brian did not see the little girl.	☐	☐

CHAPTER 4

Chinese New Year

9 This was the Year of the Dragon. The Chinese believe that the dragon brings good luck.

The Chinese New Year Parade is a very big event in San Francisco. It always takes place on a Saturday night between January 21 and February 19. The date depends on the position of the moon. Thousands of people go to see the parade every year. There are many beautiful costumes, Chinese music and Grant Avenue is decorated with colorful lanterns.[1] A long paper dragon moves along Grant Avenue. There are firecrackers[2] and lots of noise.

Jim and Brian took the cable car to Grant Avenue. It was always fun to ride the cable car. Susan and their high school friends were at the parade. Jenny Lee was there with her new boyfriend. He was the captain of the football team and he was handsome. There was a big crowd everywhere. Suddenly, on the

1. **lanterns** : 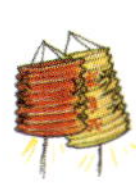

2. **firecrackers** : 

other side of the street Jim saw the face of the little girl at the window in the crowd.[1] Jim told Brian.

"Let's follow her," said Brian.

It was difficult to move because there were lots of people everywhere. Then the big paper dragon appeared in the parade. The little girl suddenly disappeared behind the long dragon.

1. **crowd** : a lot of people together in one place.

"How can anyone disappear so quickly?" said Jim. They went back to watch the parade. "Maybe she *is* a ghost," he thought.

The weekend passed quickly. It was Monday morning and they were at school. Brian and Jim told Susan about the girl. Now she wanted to explore the Stewart mansion too. They made plans during lunch.

"Let's go this evening after dinner. Remember to bring a flashlight [1] and wear dark clothes," said Jim.

They were very excited. When school finished at 3.15 p.m. they ran out. They wanted to go home quickly. At about 7 p.m. they met in front of Jim's house on Telegraph Hill.

When they arrived at the Stewart mansion everything was dark. It was a foggy, windy night. They looked at the window on the second floor, but there was no one there. They climbed over the fence and went into the garden. The tall trees moved in the wind.

"I don't smell anything this time," said Susan.

"Me neither," agreed Jim.

"And now what do we do?" asked Brian.

"I don't know," said Jim.

"Let's look inside. There are windows near the ground," said Susan. "And let's remember to be very quiet," she whispered.

"OK," said Jim.

The three friends went to a window and looked inside. The glass was old and dirty. Brian turned on his flashlight and looked. There was a small room with an old desk and some chairs.

"This was probably the study," said Brian.

Susan turned on her flashlight. "Look at the newspaper on the desk," said Susan. "I can't see well, but it I think it's yesterday's

1. **flashlight** : 

newspaper. Look at the headline: [1] 'Water scarce [2] in San Francisco'."

"But no one lives here," said Jim.

They looked inside another window and saw a big room with old furniture. It looked like the living room. On the wall there was a big painting of a man, a woman and a little girl.

"Look, that's probably a painting of the Stewart family," said Susan.

"Yes, before the mysterious accident," said Jim.

"And the little girl has long, dark hair. She looks like the girl at the window," said Susan.

"But we saw the little girl at the parade," said Brian. "How can she be a ghost?"

"Remember, she disappeared behind the dragon very quickly," said Jim.

They went to the other side of the mansion. There was a broken window [3] near the bottom of the house. They looked inside. They saw a big dark basement. [4] No one was there. Then Jim turned on his flashlight too. In the basement they saw some long tables. There were test tubes, [5] glass bottles and other laboratory equipment.

"This looks like our chemistry lab," said Jim.

"Maybe someone is using it," said Susan. "But why?

"Maybe someone is experimenting... with something secret," said Brian.

"I don't like this place," said Susan. "It gives me a bad feeling."

"Are you scared?" asked Brian.

"No, I want to come back again, but in the daytime," said Susan.

"OK," said Jim. "Let's go then."

1. **headline** : a title of a story in a newspaper.
2. **scare** [skeəs] : not available in large amounts.
3. **broken window** : the window was in pieces.
4. **basement** : a room under a house.
5. **test tubes** : 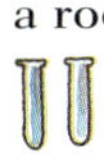

Mystery in SAN FRANCISCO

Crash! There was a loud noise. It came from one of the rooms upstairs.

"What was that?" cried Susan.

"We're not alone here. Someone or something is here," said Jim.

"Let's get out of here!" said Brian. They started running to the fence. They ran under the trees and suddenly heard a strange sound from the branches [1] above their heads. They looked up.

"Eek!" cried Susan. "Bats!"

They climbed over the fence quickly and ran away.

1. **branches** : 

UNDERSTANDING THE TEXT

KET

1 **Read the paragraph below and choose the best word (A, B or C) for each space (1-8).**

The Chinese New Year parade is an important 0....B.... in San Francisco. There 1.......... beautiful costumes and colorful lanterns. There is also 2.......... of noise. A long paper dragon moves 3.......... Grant Avenue. Jim and Brian 4.......... the cable car to Chinatown and had fun. 5.......... the parade they saw the face of the little girl at the window. They followed 6.......... but it was difficult to move. Suddenly the little girl disappeared 7.......... the long dragon. So they continued 8.......... the parade.

0	A engagement	(B) event	C matter
1	A be	B is	C are
2	A lots	B much	C many
3	A at	B by	C along
4	A held	B took	C brought
5	A At	B For	C Of
6	A she	B her	C it
7	A behind	B front	C back
8	A seeing	B looking	C watching

2 **SUMMARY**

Choose the correct words for each sentence. Then put the sentences in order to make a summary of the second part of Chapter Four.

a. ☐ In the *living room/dining* room there was a painting on the *window/wall.*

b. ☐ Susan, Brian and Jim put on *dark/new* clothes and brought a *radio/flashlight.*

c. ☐ They saw a *book/newspaper* on the *desk/floor.*

d. ☐ A loud *voice/noise* came from a room *upstairs/downstairs.*

e. ☐ They climbed *over/under* the *fence/gate* and went into the mansion.

f. ☐ They met *in front of/behind* Jim's house at 7 p.m.

g. ☐ There was *laboratory/sports* equipment in the dark basement.

Try and continue the story. Write three more sentences.

3 WRITING

Complete Brian's diary with words from the box.

basement fence flashlight mansion
newspaper noise painting place

Monday, February 10

Today was cool. Susan, Jim and I went to the old **1**.................. Jim discovered so we could explore. It was really scary. All foggy and dark. We climbed over the **2**.................. and went in.
I turned on my **3**.................. . We saw an old study and Susan saw a **4**.................. on a desk. There was a big **5**.................. of the Stewart family in the living room! Then we discovered a dark **6**.................. with a chemistry lab. We were really scared when we heard a loud **7**.................. in the mansion so we ran away. What a scary **8**..................!

BEFORE YOU READ

1 **Listen to the first part of Chapter Five and decide if the sentences are true (T) or false (F).** (10)

	T	F
1. The child's voice came from inside the mansion.	☐	☐
2. The man touched Jim's hand.	☐	☐
3. The man was not happy to see Jim.	☐	☐
4. He had long, gray hair.	☐	☐
5. Jim didn't recognize the man.	☐	☐
6. The man was around forty years old.	☐	☐
7. The man was dangerous.	☐	☐

2 **What do you think happens next? Discuss with the class.**

CHAPTER 5

A Mysterious Magician

10 Jim heard the voice of a child in the fog.

"Help! Help!"

It was a cold night. Jim stood in front of the Stewart mansion. There was fog everywhere.

The voice came from inside the mansion. He didn't know what to do. He wanted to help the child, but he also wanted to run away.

Suddenly he felt a hand on his arm. For a moment his heart stopped. He could not turn around. He was too scared.

An angry voice behind him said, "What do you want?"

Jim turned around slowly. He saw a big man with long, dark hair and angry eyes. "It's the same man I saw at the supermarket two weeks ago," he thought.

He was about fifty years old. He had a silver tooth and it

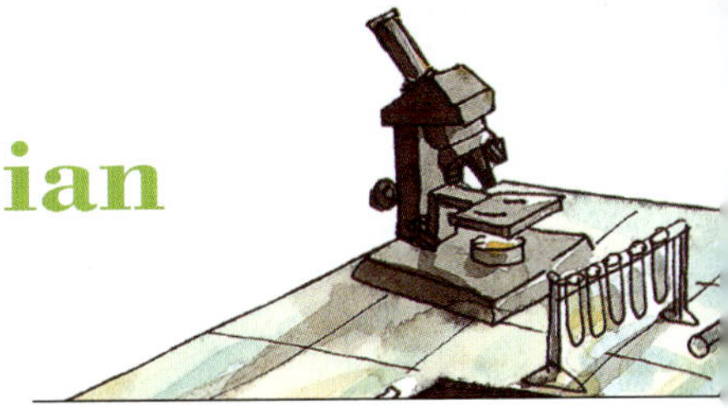

shone [1] in the dark. He also had a silver earring. He was awful. "Well, what do you want here?"

Jim looked at him and said, "Noth... nothing... Who are you?"

"Don't ask questions. Stay away from here. I'm a dangerous man. I eliminate problems and you're a problem. Go away *now*."

He pushed Jim to the ground and disappeared in the fog.

Jim woke up. He was scared.

"Phew! [2] It was only a dream," he thought. He looked at his alarm clock. It was 3 a.m.

The next day Jim, Brian and Susan went back to the mansion in the afternoon. They went to the basement window. No one was there. But there was a big black book on one of the tables.

"Someone was here last night or this morning. There's a book on the table. It wasn't here last night," said Jim.

"You're right!" said Brian.

"And *who* has the keys to the mansion?" asked Susan.

"That's a good question," said Brian.

The days passed and something else happened. The grass in Washington Square was green again and there were flowers! Everyone in the neighborhood was surprised and happy.

Jim talked with his grandfather about this.

"Grandpa, it's amazing. Washington Square is beautiful again. The grass and the flowers are growing. But how? There's no rain. How can grass and flowers grow without water?" said Jim.

1. **shone** : (shine, shone, shone) gave out bright light.
2. **Phew** [fjuː] : Jim uses this expression because he is happy it was only a dream.

3 LANGUAGE PRACTICE

Which notice (A-H) says this (1-5)?

0 Your parents can come here at 8 p.m. (C)
1 You can't mail a letter here every day.
2 Keep the park clean.
3 You can buy a French dictionary here.
4 You cannot take dogs inside this building.
5 You cannot buy tickets in the afternoon.

A
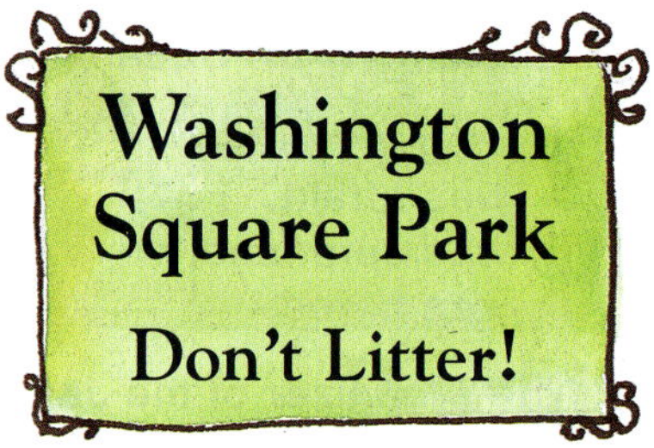

E

B
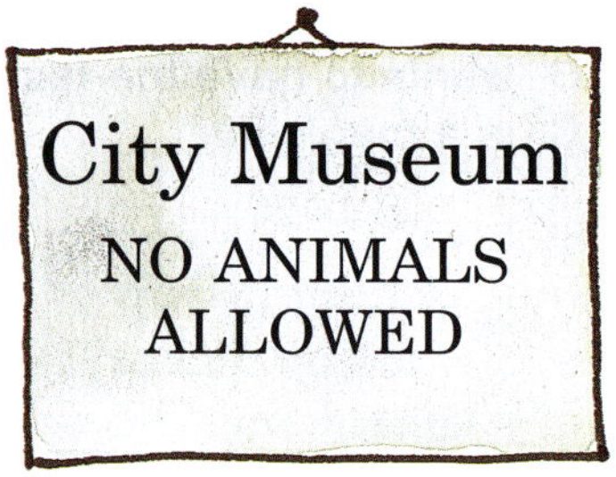

F

C

G

D

H

CHAPTER **6**

The Game

11 One afternoon Susan took the Moreno children to Washington Square. They played in the small playground. Then they went to the duck pond. The children liked feeding the ducks in the pond. But the ducks were not hungry.

"Susie, why aren't the ducks eating the bread?" asked little Sally Moreno.

"I don't know. It's strange. They're usually hungry. The fish aren't hungry either," said Susan. "Well, it's half past five and it's time to go home."

The next morning there was a big crowd at Washington Square. Jim, Brian and Susan were there with many other people. Everyone was at the duck pond. Some of the ducks were dead and others were sick. Lots of fish were dead too.

"This is terrible," said Susan.

Mystery in SAN FRANCISCO

"Someone poisoned [1] those poor ducks," said Jim.

At that moment the bus came and the students got on. On the bus everyone continued talking about the ducks.

Early the next morning Jim's grandfather bought the newspaper. During breakfast this is what they read:

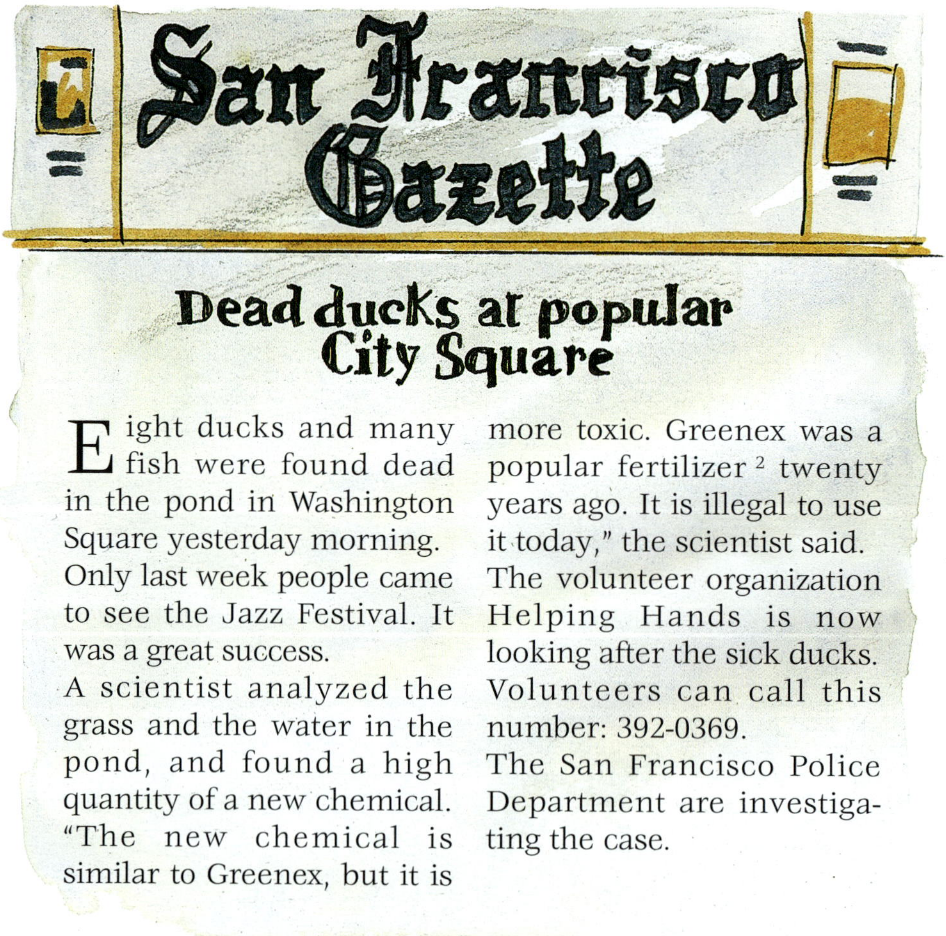

San Francisco Gazette

Dead ducks at popular City Square

Eight ducks and many fish were found dead in the pond in Washington Square yesterday morning. Only last week people came to see the Jazz Festival. It was a great success.

A scientist analyzed the grass and the water in the pond, and found a high quantity of a new chemical. "The new chemical is similar to Greenex, but it is more toxic. Greenex was a popular fertilizer [2] twenty years ago. It is illegal to use it today," the scientist said.

The volunteer organization Helping Hands is now looking after the sick ducks. Volunteers can call this number: 392-0369.

The San Francisco Police Department are investigating the case.

1. **poisoned** : gave a dangerous substance.
2. **fertilizer** : this substance helps plants to grow.

The Game

"Wow!" exclaimed Jim. "This mysterious new chemical is responsible for the green grass. So someone created a new fertilizer and it's toxic."

"What irresponsible people," said Jim's grandfather. "Think of the children. They play in Washington Square."

On Thursday evening Jim and Brian were at Susan's house.

"This fertilizer thing is so strange. Maybe it's a mad scientist," said Brian.

"Maybe they can make a lot of money with this new fertilizer," said Jim.

"Yes, a lot of money. And they'll poison all the animals," said Brian.

Susan was quiet for a few minutes, then she said, "I want to solve this mystery. I think there's a connection between the Stewart mansion and this fertilizer, but I don't know..."

On Friday evening Susan went to see her brother's football game. It was San Francisco University versus Monterey University. Tom was a good player. The stadium was almost full. Susan found a good seat to watch the game.

Susan liked football games. She always went to watch her brother play. It was a cold night and she put her hands in her pockets. "I'm glad I have a warm jacket," she thought. Then she looked at her watch. It was almost half past eight. It was time for the big game to start. She was excited.

Suddenly two people behind her started talking about Washington Square. But she could not hear all of their conversation because there was lots of noise. She listened carefully.

"...can't test anymore... not now..." said one young woman.

"...too dangerous..." said the other.

"These people know something," thought Susan. She continued listening but she did not look at them.

"...it's illegal... but the experiment... almost finished..." said one voice.

"...alright... on Lombard Street..." said the other voice.

"Lombard Street! The Stewart mansion is on Lombard Street. So there *is* a connection between the mansion and Washington Square," Susan thought.

Suddenly she understood. "I must tell Jim and Brian," she thought. She was very excited and looked at her watch.

The game finished on time and San Francisco University won. After the game she phoned Jim. She told him about the conversation between the two young women.

"You're a great detective Susan. You're right. It's that secret laboratory," said Jim.

"Let's tell police immediately," said Susan.

"Yes, that's the right thing to do. Tomorrow's Saturday. Let's meet early in the morning," said Jim. "I'll call the supermarket and tell them I can't work."

"OK," said Susan. "I'll call Brian now."

"It was lucky I went to Tom's football game," she thought.

UNDERSTANDING THE TEXT

KET

1 **Are the following sentences "Right" (A) or "Wrong" (B)? If there is not enough information to answer "Right" (A) or "Wrong" (B), choose "Doesn't say" (C).**

0 The Moreno children wanted to feed the ducks in the pond.
(A) Right B Wrong C Doesn't say

1 There were fifteen ducks in the pond.
A Right B Wrong C Doesn't say

2 Scientists found a dangerous chemical in the water in the pond.
A Right B Wrong C Doesn't say

3 The name of a new fertilizer is Helping Hands.
A Right B Wrong C Doesn't say

4 Tom played on the Monterey University football team.
A Right B Wrong C Doesn't say

5 At the stadium Susan heard two people talking about Washington Square.
A Right B Wrong C Doesn't say

6 The football team played for an hour.
A Right B Wrong C Doesn't say

7 The women lived on Lombard Street.
A Right B Wrong C Doesn't say

8 After the game Susan phoned the police.
A Right B Wrong C Doesn't say

2 **WORD SQUARE**

These words are connected to Washington Square:

ducks fertilizer festival fish flowers grass
landmark playground rain water

Can you find them in the word square? Circle them in red. How are they connected? Write a sentences using each one.

G	Y	P	L	A	Y	G	R	O	U	N	D	B
M	F	I	S	H	R	Y	R	F	L	A	F	A
L	G	E	G	P	F	U	A	W	Z	G	E	K
A	V	D	S	K	Y	O	I	K	M	G	R	V
N	P	S	R	T	D	V	N	I	P	R	T	J
D	Y	F	A	D	I	F	W	J	E	A	I	C
M	I	G	Z	R	H	V	M	T	U	S	L	G
A	D	U	C	K	S	N	A	R	C	S	I	U
R	E	T	S	M	K	W	U	L	O	H	Z	B
K	N	F	L	O	W	E	R	S	V	R	E	D
X	B	D	U	Z	S	K	J	O	E	V	R	Z

BEFORE YOU READ

3 13 **Listen to Chapter Seven. Are the following sentences true (T) or false (F)?**

	T	F
1. Jim, Brian and Susan went to the police station on Sunday morning.	☐	☐
2. They talked to Sergeant Chan.	☐	☐
3. He did not believe their story.	☐	☐
4. Jim lived on Lombard Street.	☐	☐
5. Jim met his friends and the policemen at 5 o'clock.	☐	☐
6. Jim went inside the mansion.	☐	☐
7. There was the smell of sulphur outside the mansion.	☐	☐
8. The policemen climbed over the gate.	☐	☐

BEFORE YOU READ

1 **Look at the pictures. Match the words to the pictures.**

1. air pollution	2. water	3. soil	4. wildlife	5. forest

Natural Resources and Pollution[1]

Natural resources are the most important things on our planet. We cannot live without them. There are many kinds of natural resources: light, air, water, soil, plants and wildlife are all natural resources.

Water is an essential natural resource. Water is becoming scarce and many people continue to waste[2] it, especially in Western countries. In many countries people do not have enough. Sometimes people die in these countries because they cannot find clean water to drink.

Air is another essential natural resource. Cars, factories and toxic chemicals all create air pollution. Pollution damages the quality of our air, especially in big cities. This means that some children and adults have problems when they breathe. Air pollution also contaminates the rain because of the large quantity of acid. Acid rain can destroy forests.

1. **pollution** : contamination of the environment.
2. **waste** : use in excess when not necessary.

Our plants and wildlife are in danger too. Trees give us the oxygen we breathe. But people do not always respect our forests or wildlife. People cut down many trees every year to make paper and other things. When we use pesticides [1] they go into the soil. This is dangerous because we eat foods from soil.

Fires can also destroy plants and wildlife. Some people are careless and create fires. Sometimes these fires burn for several days. They destroy trees and kill a lot of animals and birds.

So if we want to help conserve our natural resources, we must be careful and look after the environment. We must not use too much water. When we are outside we must not drop things in the street or throw things in rivers or in the sea. Remember, we can help conserve our natural resources only when we work together.

2 Are these statements true (T) or false (F)? Correct the false ones.

	T	F
a. There are only a few kinds of different natural resources.	☐	☐
b. Some people waste a lot of water.	☐	☐
c. Pollution levels are higher in the country than in the city.	☐	☐
d. Acid rain destroys the sea.	☐	☐
e. Oxygen comes from trees.	☐	☐
f. Many fires start because people aren't careful.	☐	☐

1. **pesticides** : artificial chemicals. These help plants grow.

CHAPTER 7

The Police **Station**

13 On Saturday morning Jim, Brian and Susan went to Chinatown Police Station.

"Good afternoon," Brian said to the policeman at the door.

"What can I do for you?" asked the policeman.

"We want to report something," said Brian.

"Come to my office and sit down," said the policeman. "I'm Sergeant Chan."

They explained everything to Sergeant Chan. He was interested and a little surprised.

"Why were you at the Stewart mansion?" asked Sergeant Chan.

"One day I saw the face of a little girl at the window," said Jim. "I told my friends and we wanted to explore it."

"Did you see anyone inside this 'secret lab'?" asked Sergeant Chan.

"No, we didn't," said Jim.

The Police Station

"I understand," said Sergeant Chan. "The mansion is very close to Washington Square. Perhaps you discovered something interesting that night. I'll send some officers to investigate. I want you to come too. You know where the laboratory is. I'll phone you."

"Yes, Sergeant," answered Jim.

In the afternoon the phone rang at Jim's house.

"Hello, this is Sergeant Chan of the San Francisco Police Department. May I speak to Jim Reilly?"

"This is Jim Reilly. Hello Sergeant Chan."

"Jim, my officers and I are going to investigate the Stewart mansion. Can we meet you at 5 o'clock this afternoon?"

"Of course. Let's meet in front of my house at 325 Lombard Street. Then we can go together," said Jim.

"You and your friends wait outside your house. We'll go in a police car," said Sergeant Chan. "We'll see you at 5 o'clock then. Goodbye."

Jim was excited. He told his grandfather about the phone call.

"I'm very proud [1] of you and your friends. You're doing the right thing," said his grandfather. He smiled, but he was worried.

"Thanks, grandpa."

Jim called Brian and Susan. "Meet me outside my house. The police are going to drive us to the mansion."

It was 5 p.m. Jim saw two police cars in front of his house. He and his friends got into the police car with Sergeant Chan.

"Good evening. This is Sergeant Lopez," said Sergeant Chan.

"Pleased to meet you, sir," said Jim, Brian and Susan.

1. **proud** : pleased and satisfied with something/someone.

"Now this is our plan. We'll drive to the mansion and my officers and I will go in. Jim, you will show us the basement window. After that you must stay outside the mansion. Only the police will enter because it can be dangerous. Do you understand?"

"Yes I do sir, I'll wait outside with my friends," said Jim.

The police car drove up Telegraph Hill. When they arrived in front of the Stewart mansion, Jim, Sergeant Chan and Sergeant Lopez got out of the car. Three policemen got out of the second car. The five men followed Jim. He took them to the gate. The policeman looked around.

"You go around the back of the house and we'll go around the front," said Sergeant Chan to the other policemen.

"Where did you see this laboratory?" Sergeant Chan asked Jim.

"Over there by the window," replied Jim.

They saw yellow smoke near the basement window. There was a bad smell like before.

"That's the smell of sulphur," said Sergeant Chan. "And it's very strong."

He opened the gate and went in. The other policemen followed him. Jim remained outside with his friends and waited.

UNDERSTANDING THE TEXT

KET

1 Read the paragraph below and choose the best word (A, B or C) for each space.

Susan, Brian and Jim went 0.....B..... Chinatown Police Station and talked to a policeman. 1............ name was Sergeant Chan. 2............ told him 3............ the Stewart Mansion. The policeman was 4............ in their story. He 5............ to investigate. He asked Jim to help. 6............ five o'clock a police car stopped 7............ Jim's house. Jim and his friends got 8............ the car and drove to the mansion.

	A	B	C
0	A in	(B) to	C at
1	A His	B He	C Him
2	A Their	B Them	C They
3	A about	B around	C in
4	A interest	B interested	C interesting
5	A deciding	B decision	C decided
6	A At	B On	C In
7	A front	B out	C outside
8	A off	B into	C on

2 GRAMMAR CHECK

Look at this sentence from Chapter Seven:

I told my friends *and* we wanted to explore it.

In this sentence *and* is a conjunction: it joins the two ideas. Complete the following sentences with one of the conjunctions from the box. Use each conjunction once.

and	but	or	so	because

1. There were many flowers in Washington Square, ... now there are none.
2. Jim was thirsty .... he drank some juice.
3. Did he play basketball .... was he too tired?
4. Yesterday Susan studied a lot .... she has an exam today.
5. They stayed home .... watched the game on television.

KET

WRITING

Susan writes an email to her best friend Kelly. Complete the email. Write one word for each space. There is an example at the beginning (0).

From:
To:
Subject:
Attachments: Photo collegue.jpg

Hi Kelly,
I've got so much **0**..to.... tell you.
Do you remember that boy I like at school, Jim? Well, I went with **1**........ and our friend Brian to explore this really old mansion on Telegraph Hill.
We discovered a secret lab **2**........ the basement. Scary! Many strange things **3**........ happening in Washington Square. Someone **4**........ testing a toxic fertilizer **5**........ the park. Now some of the ducks are dead and the fish too. It's awful.
Yesterday I **6**........ to Tom's football game. I heard **7**........ secret information about **8**........ lab. Today we're going **9**........ the Chinatown Police Station to talk to **10**........ police.
Write soon.

Love,
Susan :-)

BEFORE YOU READ

KET

1 Listen to the first part of Chapter Eight and choose the correct answer A, B, or C.

14

1 How many young people were in the laboratory?
- A four
- B two
- C three

2 How old were they?
- A about thirty
- B between twenty and twenty-five
- C twenty-three

3 The little girl was with
- A her brother.
- B her sister.
- C a man.

4 One young man and his friend
- A ran to another door.
- B ran to the window.
- C ran upstairs.

5 Barbara Dell is
- A a scientist.
- B a university student.
- C a criminal.

6 Ben Bradley
- A sleeps in the mansion.
- B works in the garden.
- C is Barbara's boyfriend.

CHAPTER **8**

The Secret **Formula**

14 There were four young people in the laboratory, two women and two men. They were in their early twenties and they were very busy with an experiment. They stood around the long table. One woman wrote something in the big black book. The other three worked with the test tubes. There was a portable computer on a small desk. Near the desk there was a little girl. The little girl was with the man with long hair and a silver earring.

Sergeant Chan looked inside the basement window and saw people in the laboratory.

"Jim Reilly was right. There *is* an illegal laboratory here. Let's go in!" said Sergeant Chan to his men.

The police broke the front door and went into the mansion. They immediately went to the basement.

"This is the San Francisco Police Department! Put your hands over your heads," Sergeant Lopez cried. "You have the right to

remain silent. Anything you say can be used against you..." [1]

The young people were surprised and angry.

Oh, no!" cried one young man. He and his friend ran to another door but the police stopped them.

"Who are you and what are you doing here? Do you know you are on private property?" said Sergeant Chan.

One of the young women spoke. She was very nervous.

"My name is Barbara Dell. We aren't criminals. We're students at San Francisco University in the Department of Chemistry."

"Who's that man? He doesn't look like a student," said Sergeant Chan.

"He's Ben Bradley. He has the key to the mansion because his grandfather was a gardener here many years ago. Now Ben doesn't have a home. He sleeps here at night," said Barbara Dell. END

"Oh, shut up!" said Ben Bradley angrily.

"Be quiet!" said Sergeant Chan. "Now continue your story."

"Don't tell them anything, Barbara!" cried one of the young men. "The formula is our secret."

"I want to tell the truth," said Barbara. "We discovered a new molecule at the university. With this molecule we created a new formula for a powerful fertilizer. People can use this fertilizer without water. We knew that no one lived in this mansion. And we knew that there was an old laboratory in the basement because Mr Stewart was a scientist. We wanted to keep this a secret because..."

"Because you wanted to sell it to a company and make a lot of

1. **You have the right to remain silent. Anything you say can be used against you** : in the USA policemen must say these things to protect the people they are arresting.

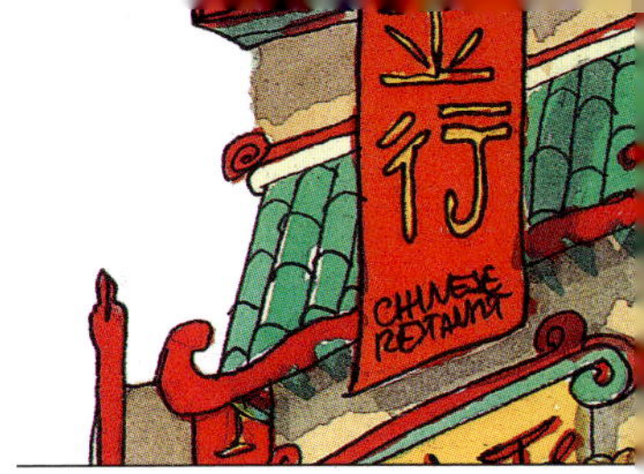

money. And you tested the fertilizer in Washington Square. You polluted the water of the duck pond. You killed the ducks and the fish. Your new fertilizer is toxic and very dangerous. Do you know that children play in the park near the duck pond?" asked Sergeant Chan angrily.

"We didn't want to pollute the water in the pond or the grass in the park," said one of the young men. "We just wanted to test the new fertilizer."

"And you decided to test it in a public park! Didn't you think about the people and the wildlife? You four must come with us to the Police Station," said Sergeant Chan. "We will also take all the chemicals you are using in this laboratory."

The little girl at the desk was scared and started crying. She ran to Barbara Dell.

"Who is she?" asked Sergeant Lopez.

"She's my little sister. I bring her here sometimes," said Barbara.

Then the policemen, the university students and Ben Bradley came out of the mansion. Jim, Brian and Susan were outside. When Jim saw Ben Bradley he was very surprised. "It's the man from the supermarket," he thought.

The little girl looked at Jim. "Well, she's not a ghost. She's real," he thought.

Sergeant Chan smiled at Jim, Brian and Susan and said, "You helped us a lot. Thank you. Come to the Police Station tomorrow and I'll explain everything. Thank you again."

The police cars drove away.

The next day the three friends went to talk to Sergeant Chan.

"Those university students were very intelligent," said Jim.

"They created a new formula."

"Yes, but they were also very irresponsible. We found many illegal chemicals in that basement. Those chemicals are very toxic. Now we must close Washington Square for a few weeks. There will be a lot of work for our chemical experts," said Sergeant Chan.

"What will happen to the university students?" asked Susan.

"There will be a trial,"[1] said Sergeant Chan. "They could go to prison."

"How are the other ducks?" asked Brian.

"The volunteers at Helping Hands are looking after them. They're feeling better," said Sergeant Chan.

Jim, Brian and Susan left the police station. They were all happy.

"Pizza for everyone tonight," said Jim.

"Great idea," said Brian.

"Let's go to Nico's Pizza Place on Washington Square," said Susan.

Jim and Brian looked worried.

"Don't worry, I'm only joking," said Susan laughing.

1. **trial** : a legal process to decide what will happen to them.

CHINESE

UNDERSTANDING THE TEXT

1 Choose the correct ending to complete these sentences.

1. ☐ Four young people
2. ☐ Sergeant Chan and his officers broke the front door
3. ☐ Ben Bradley did not have a home,
4. ☐ Barbara Dell and her friends discovered a new molecule
5. ☐ They created
6. ☐ They tested it
7. ☐ Barbara Dell sometimes brought
8. ☐ The police took the four university students
9. ☐ In the secret laboratory the police found
10. ☐ Susan, Jim and Brian were happy because

a. so he slept at the mansion at night.
b. a new powerful and toxic fertilizer.
c. a large quantity of illegal chemicals.
d. were busy with an experiment.
e. her little sister to the laboratory.
f. and went into the mansion.
g. at the university.
h. in Washington Square.
i. they solved the mystery.
j. to the Chinatown Police Station.

2 Unscramble each of the words. Copy the letters in the numbered cells to the cells with the same number to discover the mystery words.

1. MITECSYRH

6					1		5	

2. TILRA

		7	2	

3. DIILEWLF

	7					4	

4. TYEVURNIIS

		7			5				

5. NMNISAO

	2	3			8	

6. MBNESTE

	2	1				3	

1	2	3

4	5	2	3	6	7	1	6	8

EXIT TEST – PORTFOLIO

KET

1 **Are the following sentences "Right" (A) or "Wrong" (B)? If there is not enough information to answer "Right" or "Wrong", choose "Doesn't say" (C).**

1 Jim, Brian and Susan go to Galileo High School in San Francisco.
A Right B Wrong C Doesn't say

2 Washington Square is a historical landmark.
A Right B Wrong C Doesn't say

3 It is never foggy in San Francisco.
A Right B Wrong C Doesn't say

4 There are fifteen boys on Brian's basketball team.
A Right B Wrong C Doesn't say

5 Jim saw the face of a little girl at the window of the Stewart mansion.
A Right B Wrong C Doesn't say

6 Jim, Brian and Susan saw the ghost of an old man there.
A Right B Wrong C Doesn't say

7 They discovered a secret cemetery in the garden.
A Right B Wrong C Doesn't say

8 The ducks and fish at Washington Square died because of a new toxic chemical.
A Right B Wrong C Doesn't say

9 The new toxic fertilizer was responsible for the green grass at Washington Square.
A Right B Wrong C Doesn't say

10 Susan heard an important conversation at Tom's basketball game.
A Right B Wrong C Doesn't say

11 Sergeant Chan and Sergeant Lopez are thirty years old.
A Right B Wrong C Doesn't say

12 Four university students discovered a new molecule and created a new formula.
A Right B Wrong C Doesn't say

13 The police did not find any illegal chemicals in the secret laboratory.
A Right B Wrong C Doesn't say

SCORE /13

2 Complete this crossword.

ACROSS

2. When there are a lot of people in one place, we say that it is .... .
5. 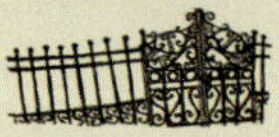
7. The money you get from a part-time job.
9. This substance helps plants grow.
10. 
12. 

DOWN

1. 
3. 
4. 
6. The title of a story in the newspaper.
8. A very big house.
11. 

SCORE /12

TOTAL /25

KEY TO THE **EXIT TEST**

1 **1** A / **2** A / **3** B / **4** C / **5** A / **6** B / **7** B / **8** A / **9** A / **10** B / **11** C / **12** A / **13** B

2 **Across: 2.** crowded / **5.** gate / **7.** pocket money / **9.** fertilizer / **10.** lantern / **12.** flashlight

Down: 1. firecrackers / **3.** dragon / **4.** silver earring / **6.** headline / **8.** mansion / **11.** bat